MW00460979

THIS BOOK BELONGS TO

Made in the USA
Columbia, SC
04 December 2022

72700788R00063